T0121515

A Wealth of Wisdom

A Reference Collection of African Proverbs

Publications by Babila Fochang

1995, *Unity is Strength*, Yaounde: Moral Guide Series,

1996, *My Son Welcome Back*, Yaounde: Moral Guide Series

1997, *Confrontations*, Yaounde: Moral Guide Series,

1998, *The Revolution that never was*, Yaounde: Moral Guide Series.

2001, *Wisdom of the Ancients*, Dschang: Dschang University Press,

2006, *Make a Daily Appointment with God*. Bali Nyonga: MMRC Publications.

2007, *Keep your Daily Appointment with God*. Bali Nyonga: MMRC Publications.

2008, *Bali Nyonga: A People without God? – An investigation into the concept of God among the Bali Nyonga People*, Bali Nyonga: MMRC Publications.

2008, *In Search of Identity and Relevance: African Reflections on Christianity*, Bali Nyonga: MMRC Publications,

Others include articles "The Spirit and spirits in African Traditional Religion and African Theology" in *Areopagus, a journal of the systematic Theology Forum of the PCC*, Vol.1, No.2, 2007

"Mission and Culture" in Dah, Jonas N, (ed.), 2008Mission in a Post-Missionary Era, Buea: PCC.

"Traditionale Religion" in Zimmermann Armin(ed.), 2008, *Evangelische Kirche in Kamerun, Das Land – die Menschen – die Kirche* ,Neuendettelsau: Erlanger Verlag für Mission und Ökumene

"Issues of Gospel and Culture" in *Areopagus, A journal of the systematic Theology Forum of the PCC*, Vol.1, No.3, 2009

"Talking of god in Everyday Life – What we can learn from Christian men and women in Cameroon", in Stebler, christoph (ed.), 2010, *Voices From Kumba, A journal of the PCC*, vol.iii

"Old Wine in New Wineskin? Social Change and Traditional Religion in Bali Nyonga", Fokwang, Jude & Kehbuma Langmia (eds.), 2011, *Society and Change in Bali Nyonga – Critical Perspectives*, Mankon, Bamenda: Langaa RPCIG

A Wealth of Wisdom

A Reference Collection of African Proverbs

Babila Fochang

Bamenda
Spears Media Press

Spears Media Press
P O Box 1151
Bamenda, NWR,
Cameroon
www.spearsmedia.com
Email: info@spearsmedia.com

Ordering Information:
Quantity sales. Special discounts are available on quantity purchases by corporations, associations, and others. For details, contact the publisher at the address above.

First published by CINRED Publications in 2013
Second Edition © 2015

ISBN: 978-1-942876-01-4

Dedicated to all lovers of wisdom

Contents

Preface

In its introduction, the 'Oxford Advanced Learner's Dictionary of Current English' states inter-alia that note should be taken that proverbs are seldom used in ordinary speech or writing. It goes on to say proverbs "...are thought of as the sort of remarks that would be made by someone who is rather dull, someone who cannot express in his own words what he thinks or feels, but who has to borrow a proverb from the language to do this. A proverb, a cliché, a truism, hackneyed phrase, and a trite remark are all sorts of expressions that someone who wants to express himself clearly, carefully and honestly will try to avoid".

On the contrary African oral literature and to some extent written literature as well sweetly embraces the use of proverbs. Proverbs to the African is a very delicious ingredient, which spices conversation, discussion and arguments.

A proverb has been defined as a "popular short saying, with words of advice or warning. John S. Mbiti thinks that proverbs are one of the areas where African philosophical systems may be formulated. Mbiti however regrets that "we do not however have many comprehensive collections of African proverbs out of which an overall analysis of this type of philosophy could be undertaken."

By 'African Philosophy' Mbiti refers to "the understanding, attitude of mind, logic and perception behind the manner in which African peoples think, act or speak in different situations of life." So to say, to understand a people's worldview it is of importance to study their proverbs.

II

To use proverbs in its rightful context one must be versed with the thought forms of a people.

With the definition we earlier had of proverbs, it may be difficult to make a clear-cut distinction between proverbs, figurative expressions, figures of speech, and idioms. This difficulty arises from the fact that what in this collection has been translated as proverbs in 'Mungaka' (the language of the Bali Nyonga) means "language (talk) of the elders or language (talk) of the 'Ti people' who to the Bali people remains symbols of wisdom.

The use of proverbs is situational. One day for example we were at a certain 'Manjong house'. One father came in just about thirty minutes late. Another elderly person told him he had missed a lot for there had been a lot of wining and dining. The father who came later just laughed and remarked: "rain water has just passed through the farm and you say the river overflowed it banks." He meant that there had been no feast; otherwise he would have met some leftover.

Even in their songs and this is especially true of dirges, proverbs are used. For example "the animal has caught me with a spear in my hand" is a dirge mourning the sudden death of a right hand person. Or when one says "I conjured rain and it has fallen on me", one is saying one has fallen into the pit he dug for others.

Proverbs equally serve, as yardsticks like when it is said, "the cock that pecked at anything did peck a glowing coal." This is cautionary against sexual promiscuity and its consequences. What is also translated into English as proverbs may simply be seen in English as metaphor. For example, when a woman tells a man that "te forest has been flooded with water", she is simply being polite in saying that she is in her menstrual period. It is equally metaphorical when in desperation one cries out that "I have the bowl in my hand, yet I am not able to fill the calabash."

It is in this light of the various forms of speech, which are all seen as proverbs in Mungaka and other African languages that I choose the title **"Wisdom of African Sages" (previously published under this title),** because all figures of speech are indicative of wit.

III

It is said that "wisdom resides with grey hairs." That is why in Bali as we saw earlier, wise words are attributed to 'old people'. The Mungaka word for an elderly person is "vuked". Literally it means one who is close to death. In other words wisdom comes with age. In this regard, I may not be the right person to produce this collection. Of course, when a child washes his hands clean, he can then eat with the elders.

My father left this world in 1976 when I was 16 years old, which now makes me 40 years old. I was forced to mingle with the elders. From the day of his death, it was known that as an only son I was to succeed him. I hesitated for the enstoolment until I was 20 years old. And even then I felt it was still too early, but I feared to delay further because "as you eat be sure you deserve it." By this you are securing your life. These are the words of a song, which scares and warns. I had therefore to deserve what was often forcefully given to me. I had to do everything to fulfil my succession. And from then I was always among elders so I gathered a lot from their discussions.

Being but a child, I had little to contribute to their conversations. I took that chance therefore to listen to them and to analyse their words.

You do not very often go asking for the interpretation of a proverb. You read its meaning from its context of use. You test its application in your daily conversation and writings. This is just what I have done.

It has taken me some 20 years to gather and test the application of this collection.

IV

The proverbs in this collection are drawn mostly from Bali Nyonga in the North Wester Region of Cameroon. It must be observed that proverbs like any other cultural values of a people cuts across ethnic, regional and geographical boundaries. While it may be that proverbs that rhyme with those of other areas may have existed independently, it is equally true that migrations, commerce, slavery, and intermarriages might have helped to exchange ideas from (or to) other areas.

Speaking in veiled language is a gift of God. In this sense, Jesus ended most of his parables (which were often proverbs which he expanded upon) with these words: "He who has ears, let him hear." Nonetheless, he took time off, very often to explain the meaning of the parables to his disciples. It is the sympathy of this handicap in others that I have attempted this noble task.

Someone has said that "every translation is a betrayal." Seen this way one recognises the difficulty of presenting a work of this calibre in English. The deep meaning and impact of some words in its original language lacks equivalence when translated. It was for this reason that while reading some of the Mungaka proverbs already complied in English by retired German missionary Rev. Johannes Stockle, I had to disagree with him. While apologising that I am not a linguist, I tried to stay close to the original meaning in my translation. It is common logic to interpret the proverbs; and this is even made easier when one studies the context, situation or circumstance in which one often heard them used.

In some instances I have simply given a corresponding English proverb in place of an interpretation. I have not classified them; neither have I made any distinction as to what Ngala Ghiantar calls "Welleric Proverbs" . These are "… proverbs which quote some animals as having said this or that."

"When we dig new a road we must cut across the existing one." This becomes the raison d'être for the collection of ancient wit and wisdom. Remember that the usefulness of proverbs to orators and animators cannot be under estimated.

(This introduction was written for the original collection that was published in 2001. In this revised edition, a new collection of proverbs from other African countries have been added to the Bali Nyonga collection).

Preface to 2nd Edition

The motivation for a second edition to this work was twofold: The first edition of the work was in short supply, so when the request for more copies kept coming I was compelled to order for a reprint. Feedback from concerned readers and my own rereading revealed some typographical errors which had to be corrected. Besides, there were repetitions of some proverbs which necessitated a revision before reprint.

My second motivation for a next edition was that I felt the need to make available the proverbs of other African countries to those who did not know that the Cameroonian proverbs bore a lot of similarities with other parts of the continent. To achieve this I gathered some through conversations with my university colleagues from various parts of the continent and gleaned some from published works which I have acknowledged in the bibliography.

I owe a debt of gratitude to my university colleagues and all who gave the necessary assistance to the realization of this edition. Special thanks to Mr. Tangwan Eric, Secretary of Presbyterian congregation of Bonaberi, who did the typing of the section of proverbs from other African countries. Our desire is that the wisdom of African forebears should continue to inspire their posterity.

Babila Fochang
17/02/2015

Part One

BALI NYONGA PROVERBS

1. Short people dance and sweat but only the tall ones are seen.
   Praise is not usually given to those who deserve them. The minors in spite of their hard work are often sidelined in honour of those who matter.
2. If you have removed the meat please allow me eat my fufu with the empty soup.
   This is sometimes directed to an unfaithful woman. The husband derides the boyfriends of his wife, or when people are fighting over something. The reserved person sits back and says they should at least leave him with the chaff after they've gotten the best part.
3. We strain for just the soup while others eat the meat.
   While other people labour to get just at the fringes, others are right at the centre.
4. When a finger stays too long in the anus, it will surely come out with excrement.
   It is good to address issues as soon as they arise.
5. When scabies come out of the buttocks, it gives work to the fingernails.
   This is in true African Communal spirit. A quiet man would still have a dreary time caused by a troublesome member of the family.
6. A child who says the mother should not sleep will not also sleep.
   It is easy to think you are making trouble for someone else. But be sure that you shall not be left out of the trouble yourself.
7. The toilet just behind the house produces a very foul stench.
   It is not good to go out with a woman just next door.
8. A child carried on the back does not know how long the journey is.

He who is dependent does not know how difficult life is.

9. A child who is carried on the mother's back cannot complain of having walked on mud.
   Those who are dependent should not complain about the hurdles of life.
10. Now that the caterpillars have left, the garden egg can now bear good fruits.
    The obstacle has been removed so let us do as we please.
11. You are merely keeping away the flies from the king's meat.
    Though you have the meat, you cannot eat it. You are merely a caretaker. This is used especially when an errand boy behaves as if the thing was his.
12. To shave a monkey you must first of all tie its hands.
    There are times you have to use coercion in order to bring a good deed to some people.
13. If you do not swell your jaws you cannot whistle.
    Nothing ventured, nothing gained. There is always an opportunity cost.
14. Do not swell your jaws for others to whistle.
    Do not give your time to labours that will be enjoyed by others at your discomfort.
15. When you are blowing fire, be sure that smoke will enter your eyes.
    When you choose to embark on an enterprise, be sure that there are obstacles, and that nothing good comes easy.
16. You cannot put water in your mouth to blow fire with.
    Do not be a job's comforter. Do not contradict an objective. You cannot say you are a trouble-shooter while at the same time you are fanning the flames of conflict.
17. It is a friendship between the fly and a corpse.
    In a one sided type friendship, only one party gains from the other.

18. You are giving medicine to a corpse.
    It is past recovery. The matter is beyond remedy.
19. Before giving (turning) your back to the fire, be sure there is somebody who will continue to kindle the flame for you.
    Unless or until you have somebody to help you, you have to do it yourself.
20. You cannot burn your fingers if you have a stick to kindle fire with.
    You cannot over labour yourself if there is somebody to assist you.
21. Never leave your hoe at home while going to the farm.
    You must eat well in order to work well.
22. When a snake bites you, you have to be wary of the millipede.
    It is good to take precautions once you've been a victim to some malaise.
23. When a man falls, he will see the need for a staff.
    Similar to 22 above.
24. If the trap was not set by you, do not happily take home the dead animal you find caught in the trap.
    It is not good to quickly take possession of what we did not labour for.
25. When you throw down somebody in a wrestling match, get off him.
    If you have proven that you are superior to the other person, be it in prowess, wealth or knowledge, you should leave the person alone.
26. A woman who desperately needs a child does not fear the size of a penis.
    When one is in desperate search of something, one does not fear any risk.
27. The woman who very much needs a child should not

deny any man.
Almost like 26 above more like a drowning man will catch at a straw.

28. The woman who is ashamed to open her legs to the midwife will die during childbirth.
If you do not expose your problems or difficulties, you will not have solutions to them.
29. Before she knew how to weep (sing dirges) all her children were dead.
Experience is the best teacher, so they say, but the lesson might come too late.
30. The fly with no one to advice it, followed the corpse into the grave.
It is always good to seek advice from others, because as John Donne puts it 'no man is an island'.
31. The palm beetle by eating the core of the palm tree does not know that by the time the palm will be dying, it too (the beetle) will also die.
The evil plan, which you have for others, is like a boomerang. The palm beetle is usually extracted from palms. People know it is inside a palm only when they see the palm suddenly withering away. They know then that it has been eaten inside by the beetle, so they now come for the beetle.
32. The animal has died in a house fire.
Something has happened to one who is equal to the task.
33. If you stay in the farm for long, you'll likely carry wet wood.
Do not wait until the last minute and then start doing things in a rush. You are bound to make mistakes.
34. Do not crack kernels on your knee.
Do not out of pride do the impossible which will be disastrous to you. It is said that a man visited his mother-in-law and the mother-in-law had a nut she wanted to crack. She had

a small stone, but no bigger one on which to place the nut before cracking. Her son-in-law to prove his manhood took the nut, placed it on his knee and starting hitting it. He wounded himself on the knee very seriously, but the nut was not cracked; hence the above saying.

35. Maize has returned from the market of fowls.
    The thing is so bad that even fools and beggars reject it.
36. The grass is for goats.
    Let it remain for whom it was made.
37. The corn remains for fowls.
    Just like no. 36
38. The grass was for the goats, but today human beings also help themselves with it.
    Unlike in 36 and 37 above, this refers to someone doing or behaving in a way that is not expected of them.
39. The bird tells the branch "before you decided to break, I was about to fly".
    A boss may decide to dismiss a worker just when the worker has taken a decision to resign.
40. If you hear the sound of mourning in a bachelor's house then he is dead.
    This is because as a bachelor he lives alone. There are certain situations where we cannot doubt what has happened.
41. If you see faeces in a bachelor's compound it must have been dropped by birds.
    Because the bachelor has no child who can throw faeces carelessly. These two sayings were meant to caution against bachelorhood.
42. If water is dirty, it is dirty right at the source.
    If the children are bad, it is because the parents are bad. If a nation is corrupt, it is because its leadership is corrupt.
43. I have a bowl in my hand, yet I am not able to fill my calabash.

This is a situation where one feels helpless even when one has the supposed means of help. This is especially true of a man who has children, but jealousy has caused others to be killing these children through witchcraft. This saying is usually sung in a dirge.

44. If a woman does not have children in her womb, she cannot give birth to her intestines.
We can only do what is within our ability. We can only give what we have.
45. The bird fell prey to the hunter's trap because of the termite (bait).
Beware of the enticements of a beautiful woman, she will lead you into a trap.
46. Do not be one who roofs people's houses yet his own roof is in serious need of repairs.
It is good for charity to begin at home; even though it should not end there.
47. There's wine in the pot, but where are those to drink?
The wine here represents a corpse. The dead person is believed to have been killed through witchcraft. If those who killed him thought it was meat, then let them eat. This is a dirge.
48. The stomach that is full does not know why the empty stomach has to complain.
Unless you have passed through certain experiences you will not know what it means when somebody is complaining of such an experience. Those who are well placed do not understand why the less fortunate actually grumble.
49. While we sympathise with dry leaves, it is the fresh ones that suddenly fall off.
We think death should take the aged, the frail, the foolish and the sicklings. Rather death chooses to take the young, the healthy, the wise and the strong.
50. Don't keep pushing me like a boundary stone.

A boundary stone is usually not planted, so it is moved from one place to the other by the land occupants. One should therefore not be made a stooge by being tossed one way or the other.

51. The world is a ridge.
    No condition is permanent in this world.
52. The gratitude of the tailless dog always goes unseen.
    The gratitude of orphans, slaves, the poor and even introverts are hardly recognisable.
53. The dog shows gratitude through its tail.
    Gratitude cannot be expressed only by word of mouth.
54. The dog should not outrun the prey in the hunt.
    There should be no haste in life. Those who are hasty often bypass their chance in life. The overtly ambitious meet with untimely ends.
55. The dog hunts not for the master, but for itself.
    Everybody is self-centered. All human beings seek self-glorification.
56. I am not a child of the late Fon.
    I have as much right to it as you do.
57. How can another man's farm produce this nice harvest?
    The world is such an envious place. Good things should not come from others. If it happens we should destroy it. This proverbial question is asked out of desperation at the death of one who meant so much to the family.
58. It is the gift of a dream.
    It came unexpected.
59. When you dig a new road, you must cut across the old one.
    Change does not mean completely doing away with the past. We need part of the old to establish a better future. A sound working premise of today should be the past.
60. There are many roads that lead to the palace.

Truth can be subjective. We may use different means or ways to arrive at the same conclusion. There is one God but many religions and many denominations by which to reach him.

61. What are fetish animals doing in the hunting area?
Fetish animals are not eaten, neither are they shot during hunting.
62. The animal is one that cannot be shot.
A man may admire a woman, but discovers that she is already married or a relative.
63. It is an animal in the trap.
It is a bird already in hand.
64. You will not develop stomach problems if you do not eat raw beans.
Trouble comes to those who go looking for it. If you are innocent, your conscience should not worry you. If you are accused falsely, there should be no cause for alarm. All will be well with you.
65. If the house does not give, the world cannot take.
Enemies can get at you only if they have conspirators within your family.
66. It is only bent, but not broken.
Though the father is dead, he has left a successor just like him.
67. 'Hearsay' causes division and quarrels.
Beware of gossips. If you depend on what they say, you will not have friends.
68. When a child strays too long at the stream, just know that the calabash is broken.
Guilt feelings will keep friends and family members away from us.
69. We thank God the water was spilled, but the calabash saved.
Even though the child passed away, (still birth) the mother's life was saved.

70. I have madc market neighbours with my enemies.
Stay alert and know that even though you are among people, you are alone.
71. Do not be too careful in avoiding mud, lest you step on excrement.
You become over careful in maintaining your integrity; yet find yourself in great scandal.
72. It is a hill race.
This is an admonishment to the young who become over hasty in the pursuit of life. Life is not only a race, but a hill race and does not need speed. Those who start a hill race at top speed hardly reach the summit.
73. Cover the faeces and remove the mushroom.
Overlook what is bad as you aim for the good.
74. If you see a giant rat by day, know that something has disturbed it.
Any unusual behaviour has some underlying cause.
75. The small monkey jumps and lands only where its mother lands
Children are what their parents are.
76. The ants cross a stream on a stick.
In any contact, there must be a middleman.
77. While you fight, listen to abuses.
One should always give an ear to side comments. It may save you from many dangers.
78. When there is commotion among the salt sellers let the oil dealers be on alert.
If people of the same interest start quarrelling, it is good for those of other interest groups to adjust.
79. If the tree does not rot, the mushroom will not grow.
It is only through a quarrel or a disagreement that you will know how the other person sees you or what he thinks of you. Bad things often produce good results.

80. The boil on another man is attractive to incise.
It is easy for us to see only the ills of others, but not ours.
81. If the wind does not blow, you cannot see the fowl's rump.
Most truths about us can only be known when certain disasters strike. For example if a supposedly wealthy man suddenly becomes bankrupt, that is when the truth about the source of his wealth will come out.
82. The animals that escape the hunters are always the ones with long horns.
We always think that the things, which passed us by, were the best.
83. This is a father's death, not a mother's.
This is an issue that needs a collective effort.
84. When many people die, people mourn only for their near kins
Though the communal life is good, when the disaster is nation-wide, one should concern oneself only with ones own family.
85. The poor man said women are witches.
We tend to ignore and abuse what is beyond our reach.
86. Do not remain waiting for the semblance of termites.
Do not waste your time chasing shadows.
87. You remain waiting for food from your favourite wife and sleep hungry.
We should accept what is available than to wait for what we love but which is not in sight. 'A bird in the hand is worth two in the bush.'
88. When you tap honey, be prepared to eat the first layer.
Whatever you undertake, be ready to accept the outcome.
89. The child who resembles neither father nor mother must have been thrown into the compound from the backyard.
This is an indirect way of saying that the mother of such a

child must have gone out with another man.

90. Only the mother knows the father of her child.
    This is because many men have received shock waves when their wives openly declared to them: 'by the way the child is not your own!'
91. The meat is one that can be eaten.
    There are no hindrances to the matter.
92. It is a dog without a bell around its neck.
    The bell on a dog's neck signifies ownership. Without a bell, the dog does not belong to anybody.
93. The dog has a bell around its neck
    This is opposed to 92 above. It is used to imply ownership of something.
94. The tiger has given birth to a bush cat.
    A strong man has given birth to a weakling.
95. Do not lick oil from a dog's ear.
    Taking from somebody to whom you ought to give.
96. Do not beg hairs from a snake.
    This is like laughing at poverty.
97. Do not seize a butterfly from a hen's mouth.
    Do not use your position to intimidate a person; or contesting something with a most junior person to you.
98. Do not remain at the funeral because you have a lot of tears.
    Avoid excesses. Do not think that because you have the ability and the powers, you must do it all.
99. Feign death to see those who love you.
    It is only when you have a problem that you can determine those who have you at heart.
100. He who did not wail, missed his father's compound.
    If you expose your difficulties, you will have solutions. The story is that a young man had been out of his village for long. His father died and when he got the news it was already

late. He came back to the village, and went to their quarter but could not determine the location of their compound. He passed by their compound some two or three times before some relatives recognised him. The idea is that had he started crying from afar, people would have joined in the crying in their compound and by this, he would have identified their compound.

101. The novice trader bought crabs.
   It is always good to seek the advice of others. On the other hand, the first fool is not a fool.
102. The semblance of termite caused division in a household.
   Do not spend your time fighting over things, which do not matter.
103. The chimpanzee that scattered so much unearthed its mother's bones.
   Do not be too inquisitive. In other words the child who seeks so much to find out how his father died wants to die the way his father died.
104. When you bend to look at somebody's anus, you expose your own to the person behind you.
   The way you treat others is the way you will be treated. Nobody is perfect.
105. The child who chose to eat only the hind leg of any animal remained waiting in vain when the father caught a python. (Mother cooked a python).
   It is good to be flexible in life. A child had insisted to his father who was a hunter that he would eat only the hind leg of any meat cooked by his mother. So on this day the father had killed a python. When they cooked it he couldn't eat because a snake has no legs.
106. The river meandered because it moved alone.
   Nobody is an island. You cannot succeed if you do not seek

advice, help or assistance.

107. It is elephant meat.

It is so big and free, for everybody or anybody to have a share. This is sometimes use to refer to women. You may have her for today, but you will not exhaust her.

108. Do not step over a crocodile to go looking for fish.

Do not be so rigid in life. Do not set your mind on a particular goal with such devotion you may bypass great opportunities.

109. If you reject the Fon, avoid his plaza.

Do not say a man is bad, yet still receiving benefits from him.

110. A ridge in the farm was not because soil was finished.

Life is fate controlled. All mishap is not due to carelessness.

111. Do not be the bride who swallowed a beetle

Do not refuse something in public, yet do it in secret. The story is that this new bride was given this delicious beetle soup. She refused and said she does not eat the beetle. Yet inwardly she had appetite for it. Meanwhile there were some of the beetles not yet prepared. And until prepared they are kept alive by putting them in a dish with salt given them as their food. In the night while people were asleep, this bride stealthily swallowed them. The beetles gnawed at here bowels and she started crying. When asked what had happened, she explained but it was too late. She died.

112. Do eat as a slave.

Slaves eat fast so as to be ready for the next assignment. In other words do not be sluggish in life.

113. I am not your toilet tissue.

Do not look low on me.

114. The wasp developed a tiny middle because it concentrated on feeding its young.

Parents should not concentrate their efforts on the welfare of children while forgetting themselves in the process.

115. The mother always locks the door with a soft bamboo.
It is good to punish the child, but the parents must always be lenient. The idea behind the saying is that although the mother may choose to lock the child outside, the lock should be one that the child can easily open to get in.

116. When mother goat grows old, it sucks the milk of its young.
We bring up children so that they can in turn help us when we are old.

117. The side of error is the side of red soil.
Red soil symbolises the grave. Any error attributed or blamed on the dead is accepted. After all, a corpse cannot defend itself.

118. Who lacks red soil behind his house?
Death affects everybody at some point. Death is not only in my family.

119. The young sucker told the plantain "get ready quick so that they can harvest you for food." Not long after the young sucker also produced plantains.
There are stages of life through which all generations must pass. Do not laugh at those who fall when there is still more slippery ground ahead. Misfortune can knock at any man's door at anytime.

120. The hen was also an egg.
Just like 119 above.

121. The strong palm front was also a young middle core.
Just like 119 and 120 above.

122. Let us see how maggots will infest the meat.
Now that the bone of contention has been removed let us see how problems will arise again.

123. If the meat does not rot, it will not smell.
When the secret leaks, the truth will be revealed.

124. It is the labour of a hen. When others are enjoying

its eggs, it starts laying more eggs.
You labour for others to enjoy.

125. You are in the house without trouble, but trouble is behind the house.
There is actually no way to escape from trouble.

126. The man who cut the bamboo has gone away, but the man who came to drag just the leaves has been caught.
The real offender is gone. The one who is accused is innocent.

127. You are mourning your dead in the market place.
Everybody is busy, so you are merely wasting your time; you will not attract any sympathy.

128. You cannot be in the house alone and complain that somebody has messed the air.
The answer to the problem is with you yourself. Do not raise a false alarm.

129. The friendship is that of the pot and the fireside.
Only one party stands to gain from such a friendship

130. The cocoyam leaf gathers rain water and throw it, not under its own stems but under another cocoyam plant.
Do not prove to the world that you have open hands, while your own family starves.

131. The grass is the ear of the Fon.
Do not gossip the Fon because everybody's ears are the Fon's.

132. If your husband dies do not marry the son of another woman, else he avenges his mother on you.
This is derived from a time when Levirate marriages were contracted. This saying is a dirge. It means old quarrels can possibly be renewed through the children.

133. Our Fon is a buffalo and we are its horns.
The strength of the Fon lies in his subjects.

134. They have distributed property and my inheritance

is the toilet.

One feels cheated by the share.

135. The testis came to escort the penis.

Destiny is accepted here. We should accept our position in life. Or some are here just as observers.

136. I will not wash my hands for others to eat the food.

You set your mind on something, but just at the nick of time you become a loser.

137. You have given birth in the year of smallpox.

Your blessing has come at an evil time. Though you have gotten it, the days are so evil and life is uncertain.

138. The conversation was too sweet and the thief laughed from his hiding place

The occasion is so joyful that even the most reserved person expresses his joy.

139. The masquerade only gives his stick to those he knows.

Those with common interest always identify with one another.

140. Do not tie your masquerade only to tell the public the person in the mask.

Do not disgrace your own person in public. Let family secrets remain within the family.

141. If your own juju has been given a fowl then do leave the arena.

The world is a stage, when you play your part, leave the stage to others.

142. When the sun is up, do your laundry.

Time waits for nobody. Simialr to "make hay while sun shines."

143. Unless it was for you, the mosquito cannot leave the forest to come and bite you.

Things await their time. Things happen as had been predestined.

144. Do not sit like a fool whose child is dead.
Always have an alert mind.

145. The road to money is thorny.
Life is not a bed of roses. Even if it was, roses grow on thorny shrubs, so to harvest a rose you are vulnerable to the piercing thorns.

146. To become rich, you must be able to sleep hungry even though you have money in the house.
You must be miserly to become rich. A spendthrift remains poor.

147. If you see a child limping because he had a wound, know that he is a stubborn child.
You will live a life of regret if you are disobedient to your parents.

148. Do not be a lion hiding your claws.
Do not pretend to be a saint, while you are a devil.

149. Hang your bag where your hand will reach.
Live within your means.

150. Do not go up the barn and take groundnuts in both hands.
Do not complicate life by doing many things at the same time. You will fail on all fronts.

151. If a woman doesn't become pregnant, she cannot give birth.
One can only give what one has. Do not expect too much from others when maybe the solution is with you.

152. If a woman does not have a child in her womb she cannot give birth to her intestines.
Certain things are beyond our grasp. Do not force somebody to do the impossible.

153. The man who had slaves grew old earlier.
You become lazy when you only expect others to serve you. Work keeps you healthy and in good shape.

154. A person's relatives and friends are his buttocks.
Your kinsmen are your backbone.

155. Do not be a cricket to call for your death.
Let trouble come if it has to, but do not go searching for it.

156. Death! What have you left in the parlour, and what do you want in the room?
Why has death not taken the old and the infirm? Why has it chosen but the young?

157. You have invoked rain, now it is falling on you!
You are reaping just what you sowed.

158. Where has the caterpillar come from to spoil the garden egg?
The feeling is that, that person should not have been the one to own it.

159. If the three fire-stones of the household are well placed, nothing will happen to the pot.
If your family members are behind you, you will be saved from outsiders.

160. Unless the house gives, the world cannot take.
Just like 161 above.

161. While waiting on somebody, it is good to be making step-by-step advances.
Do not wait for somebody while remaining at the same spot.

162. If you see flies swarming towards the same direction, be sure that there is a carcass around.
No smoke without fire.

163. Do not give corn that belongs to domestic fowls to bush fowls.
You are wasting it by giving it to those who do not deserve it.

164. Bush fowls have mixed among the domestic fowls.
It is now difficult to distinguish the good from the bad.

165. Let the cutlass not complain of pains when the tree is being felled with an axe.

Do not feel the burden of other people's responsibilities.

166. Let the dog not empty its bowels in the house because it was chained.
Do not take that as an excuse.

167. How can the young of a crocodile drown?
Where you have support, all will surely be well with you.

168. The animal has fallen into a ditch.
Now that I am trapped, enemies have an advantage over me.

169. When the animal turns its back those to shoot are many.
When you are disadvantaged even cowards take the upper hand of you.

170. Borrowed water never boils to the required degree.
You cannot depend on the things you beg from others.

171. How can I come to help you lift your load unto your head but you transfer the load on to me?
Watch out how you get mixed up in other people's business. It may cost you dearly.

172. Do not attend a funeral celebration without wine and come back with a corpse.
Become a victim of circumstance in a problem where you were not even concerned.

173. If you keep complaining of what to give, you will sever family ties.
Physical presence or mere greeting is enough.

174. If the problem is your own, you cannot give it to any one else.
What comes to us is meant for us.

175. Fingers are not the same.
Do not make comparisons.

176. The back head cannot see what is happening.
No one can know what people say about them in their absence.

177. How can we take the valley to fill the hill?

Let us not take from the man who has little to give to the man who has much.

178. A bundle of bamboo got finished because it was taken out one at a time.
No matter the quantity, if you keep on taking without replenishing, it will get finished.

179. Do not hide all your hoes in one furrow.
Do not put all your eggs in one basket.

180. Others cultivate farms and some labour vainly to keep surroundings clean.
The adulterer remains a loser. The woman remains mine. I stand to gain.

181. The forest is flooded.
A woman saying she is in her menstrual period.

182. If you cultivate an animal-infested area, you'll always be seen as a lazy person.
You may have children. But if the people hate you they'll kill them through witchcraft.

183. When the harvest is rich, you have many relatives; after the harvest they all run away.
Wealth makes your family come closer to you.

184. If you are rich, your family members cling to you, if you are poor they all run away.
The meaning is the same as in 183.

185. The cocoyam is like the paste.
Like father, like son.

186. "Had I had known" is uttered when it is too late.
It is good to think before acting.

187. A man's character is his wealth.
If you are upright, though poor, you'll never be in want.

188. You can kill a cow and eat for twenty years.
If you share with others, they will live to remember your generosity for many years to come.

189. There is a rich harvest of egusi pods to the man without fingers.
Good things come to those who do not know how to use them.

190. When you give birth on dry land, you use urine to wash the blood.
In tight circumstances, use what is available.

191. The thorn of love knows no pain or cost.
Reciprocal love knows no pain or cost.

192. Chew well before swallowing.
Know the facts well before recounting the tale to others.

193. You must shoot the bird before you wear the feather.
Prioritize your tasks.

194. The fly does not settle on a place without a reason.
There is no smoke without fire.

195. When you pick kolanuts you must look up to see if there is a kolanut tree.
It is always good to give thanks to God for your blessings. Show gratitude for what you receive.

196. Unannounced rain has fallen on me.
It has happened so suddenly. Disaster has struck so suddenly.

197. Do not hold a snake by its middle.
Beware how you tackle the matter, lest you expose yourself to danger.

198. Eat with him with a long spoon.
Take precautions with those you do not trust.

199. A house is only good when there is somebody in it.
Do not boast of your property; rather boast of your people.

200. The talkative bird never builds a nest.
Those who talk much do very little.

201. If a thorn in the house pierces you, you are gone.
If you have enemies within the family, you'll easily be brought down.

202. The river (stream) is big only because of the rivulets

(streamlet).
Even the small members of your kin are instrumental to your success.

203. The child fell from the hands of its baby sitter.
It is good that you are the person who has destroyed the very thing you hold dear.

204. The man who was ashamed ate poison.
It is good to make your intentions known on the issue at stake. Otherwise because of shame you act against your conscience.

205. Do not fear the Fon's eye and eat fufu with what you detest.
Do not do what displeases you just because you want to impress those who are superior to you.

206. A dead animal does not hear the bell of the dog.
When you are to get into trouble, you do not heed the warnings dished out to you by others.

207. There is nothing in the groundnut shell.
It is not as good as seen from face value. Not all that glitters is gold.

208. Tab, tab and the pot is full.
Little drops of water make a mighty ocean.

209. The food is not well prepared; the orphans will have their fill.
A disappointment to the fortunate ones, becomes a blessing for the less fortunate ones.

210. It is much, so the have-nots can have a share.
We are often known to be charitable, but it is just because our cups overflow.

211. The toad is wasting the termite.
They have given it to one who does not know its use.

212. The man who has a running stomach is not afraid of darkness.
Difficulties make us bold.

213. I was asked to take and keep and I became the victim.
Watch out how you meddle in other people's business, you may run into trouble.

214. The ears do not grow longer than the head.
Respect for elders and hierarchy is a prerequisite to a good life.

215. Any head rests on its own shoulder.
There are certain things which we do, and whose repercussions we alone can bear. No one can help us.

216. I washed my hands but missed the food.
Preparing with eager expectation for a thing but misses it in the end.

217. A rich man lacked a needle to stitch his bag.
Do not think that because you are self-sufficient, you cannot be in want.

218. It is good to take shelter when the rain clouds begin to gather.
It is good to take precautions to avert disaster rather than to wait for the disaster before looking for solutions. A stitch in time saves nine.

219. A big bamboo forest never lacks a dry bamboo.
An industrious person can't be in need. The more children one has, the greater the possibility of a good child from among them.

220. You cannot go to see whether the trap has caught a game if you did not set the trap.
You can only go to the farm to harvest if you planted. Do not reap where you did not sow.

221. The goat eats grass where it is tethered.
Our livelihood comes from what and where we are engaged.

222. The rain has a bad name.
We see nothing good that somebody does, no matter how hard he tries. Rain is blamed when it falls and it is equally blamed

when it does not.

223. The fowl that sleeps outside has learned all the tricks of escaping animals of prey.
Circumstance and experience improve our talents.

224. A bad animal empties its faeces at the source of the river.
Good for nothing people love high places and good things.

225. There is no "manjong" where people do not eat the head of a goat.[1]
There is always some sacrifice in any engagement. On the other hand there must be privileges for special people.

226. The man who builds by the roadside buries an unknown corpse.
Being too hospitable can lead one into trouble.

227. A drum carver dies and only half calabashes are played at his funeral.
A man who does well to other people, but the same is not reciprocated when he needs it.

228. A single tree does not become a forest.
Do not exaggerate what you possess.

229. When you bury truth here, it surfaces there.
Truth shall prevail.

230. A child does not remain like that forever.
The child would grow too.

231. A brave warrior is known only in the field of battle.
Idle boasting is not good. Boasting should be seen through action.

232. A good workman is proven only at the job site
Just like above.

233. When your brother is up the palm tree, you'll eat ripe nuts.

---

1 Manjong is a social group intended mostly for entertainment and dancing. Membership sort of defines the social status of individuals.

This is to demonstrate kinship affinities and tribal solidarity. If you have people in high places, you will surely receive the favours you seek.

234. When you rob the Fon's head (back), it will be known by your legs.
There is always some kind of reward for the services you render to others.

235. If you are drowning, you must drink some of the water.
If you have charge of food or drink, you'll surely consume some of it.

236. Do not dip your hand into the oil vessel and come out clean.
Try to have something to show for your labours.

237. When the oil changes container, it can no longer be full.
The successor cannot act in the way as the father himself.

238. We can only eat together when we work together.
If you expect to share in the sweet, you should equally share in the sweat.

239. Sharing is good to be done in the farm.
It is good that we settle with the matter while it is still early.

240. Inequality in sharing severs family bonds.
To keep our family members, and friendship we should be just in our dealings with them.

241. If your witchcraft is in water you cannot drown.
Where you have people, nobody can plot evil behind your back. You'll discover the conspiracy.

242. There's no ingredient, only the cup smells.
It is merely a reflection of the reality.

243. One hand cannot tie a bundle.
Unity is strength.

244. What is in the head of the antelope is the same in

the deer's head.
We are all made of the same stuff. Today may be mine, but next day shall be yours.

245. The same fate that befell the cocoa awaits the coffee.
Do not think that it is only for me. Misfortune comes to everybody at one time or the other.

246. Everything awaits its day.
It happens just as was foreordained.

247. When it is time, it is bound to happen.
Predestination is unavoidable.

248. It is only God who charts one's destiny.
Do not boast that you have an edge over me. Do not think you can kill me; if you do, God has willed it.

249. The left hand washes the right and the right hand washes the left before both hands can be clean.
Unity is strength

250. Your hill is full of many insects.
You like to complain. You are a grumbler.

251. To be lonesome is trouble.
No man is an island. Do not work or live in isolation.

252. It's good to be a pair when one is in error, the other one corrects him.
Two heads are better than one.

253. Because of the redness of its eyes, people accused the weaverbird that it was the one that ate the pepper.
Your speeches, behaviour, attire can often bring suspicion on you in the case where a crime is committed; though you are innocent.

254. It's better to be less cooked than to be burnt.
Half bread is better than none.

255. Goodness lasts forever.
It is good to be kind, tender hearted, generous, and hospitable.

256. I was saved from small pox only to die of measles.

One escapes from a grave danger only to become the victim of an insignificant threat.

257. Let's support the plantain while it is up.
Prevention is better than cure.

258. Once a woman is pregnant she will surely give birth or miscarry
Following natural order certain things are bound to and will surely happen. Do not hurry it up..

259. Whatever is hot will become cold.
Troubles do not last forever

260. The sun that rise surely has to set.
Life moves onward towards an end. We as youths should not despise old age. We shall be old too one day. We are born and we shall die.

261. When a cock crows it is testing the limits of its sovereignty.
It is often good to test to see how far our authority stretches.

262. An elder does not open cobs to see if the corn is strong.
Fathers should not follow girls the age of their own daughters.

263. Respect begins from the home.
You can only be respected in society if you have such respect from your own family.

264. Fools are food for the wise.
The wise profit from the folly of fools. A fool may make money; it takes the wise to spend it.

265. Who will live forever?
Do not mock somebody who is deceased. We are all mortals.

266. Speak of others' children as your own.
Do not think good only of your own children. The other person's child is as good as your own.

267. The fools' share is their mouth.
He lives to eat and talk. Apart from that he is good for

nothing.

268. Words are like arrows, once shot can never return.
Weigh your words before you utter them; for once spoken cannot be retrieved.

269. The thing with the Fon's work is that one should not be absent.
It is not good to be absent when there is communal work. You work very little. If you absent you are subject to a heavy fine.

270. The good thing belongs to the rich man.
This is because he can have what he likes, but the poor man can only like what he has.

271. I missed the animal and shot the dog.
I missed the target and instead destroyed something precious.

272. One's finger cannot piece one's eye.
One cannot harm one's family member.

273. I hid it in the bush, but the dog carried it away.
Hide it from death, yet death snatches it all the same. On the other hand it is a reward for greed.

274. One's hand cannot deceive him.
Be industrious and you will surely enjoy the fruits of your labour.

275. One's parents are one's gods.
Honour your parents.

276. If you tune a song and people answer well, you will be called a good singer.
It is by sheer luck that you have good children. It is not that you could bring them up better than others.

277. I have seen a goat in your compound whose species I admire. I have come to beg for its young to go and rear.
This is the language of betrothal. You are asking a father for the hand of his daughter in marriage.

278. I have seen a nice plantain here, I have come to beg

for its sucker.
Same like 277 above.

279. Your fowls have mixed with mine. Can you please just tell me how much I'll reimburse you for it.
This is in the case where the marriage was by elopement. You now come to reveal yourself and to bargain the bride price.

280. If you do not find your chicken, please know that I am the thief.
The same as 279 above.

281. I have come to beg for a calabash here to use in carrying water.
Same like 277and 278.

282. The bowl becomes ashamed when it realises that the basket is able to hold water.
Some people look highly upon themselves. They see others as misfits. They think that there are certain things the so-called misfits cannot do. But they become bitter when the so-called misfits excel and do even better than the best.

283. A man has an opportunity to kick your buttocks only if you are in front of him.
If somebody is envious of you, it is because you are above him. He has an inferiority complex.

284. Do not be a grown up before crawling like a monkey.
Usually a child crawls before standing. Do not be a grown up before resorting to childish pranks and behaviour.

285. Do not catch the fowl on the day of roasting.
It is good to plan your affairs well in advance.

286. I have joined the dance when the drummers are tired.
I have come when all the good things have been enjoyed. I have only met with the crumbs.

287. Before the termites come out of their hole, they

always hold a meeting.

If we belong to the same group, we should not show our disagreement in public. We must at least agree on what to do or say before meeting the public.

288. When you point a finger at somebody, many fingers point back at you.

The fault you see in others is worst in you.

289. The egg is a fowl.

Do not despise condoling with somebody who loses a baby and expect him to condole with you when you lose an adult.

290. The fowl was once an egg.

Youth should not laugh at old age. The old were once young.

291. You do not cross the bridge until you come to it.

Adolescents should wait for the right time. Do not hurry in life. Things should be done when one is ripe for them.

292. Words are like ash, once scattered cannot be gathered.

Just like 268 above.

293. The cricket thought it had been made king because the ants carried it.

We have to be cautious of some of the honours bestowed upon us. They are not usually to our advantage. The cricket when carried by the ants did not stop to ask why. It just started shouting on the ants, giving them orders, because it thought they had made it their king. Not long however, one leg was gone, another and soon there was no cricket.

294. Only those who go to Mudika, know the price of crayfish (Njanga).[2]

The matter can best be known by those who are involved.

295. Only the crab knows where its wife's private part is located.

---

2 Mudika is a seaside town in the South West Region noted for trade in smoked fish.

It is best known by the owner.

296. It is a Baba man's rain.

"Much ado about nothing". That which looks so threatening might not be so portentous afterall . The story goes that a man from Baba was coming back from the farm with his pregnant wife. A threatening rain-cloud gathered and there was every indication that a wild storm was on its course. The woman was heavy with child, so she could not move fast. To help her, so that they should hurry to reach a home for shelter before the storm, the man took his knife tore open the woman's womb to remove the child and carry it. In his naivety, he killed both wife and baby. And of course the rain did not fall.

297. Ntanbmtutu's night has befallen me.

This is a cry of desperation. It has happened so suddenly. Ntanbmutu is the day before Bali market day. As I gathered in my research, it was in 1947 that an eclipse of the sun was experienced. And this day was a Ntanbmutu. People were surprised to see night during broad daylight. It is said that after this incident Church houses were packed full, because people were convinced that the world was coming to an end.

298. Our friendship is like that of the cocoyam and the plantain.

You hide your own things from me, while I expose mine to you.

299. Do not complain that smoke is entering your eyes if you have chosen to burn wet firewood.

The repercussion of your actions will bounce back on you.

300. We have enjoyed the dance, but we cannot shake hands. We are like opposing walls.

We are condemned to live together but not to enjoy the company of one another.

301. Do not live like cashew nuts.

It is not good for members of the same family to live apart.

(The cashew nuts have separate compartment though one shell).

302. You are a cat.
You are discreet in your affairs. (Nobody sees where the cat defecates or where it copulates).

303. You are like water. No matter how they cut you, there is no wound.
You are a hard bone to crack. People find it difficult to discover your weak points.

304. Let your journey not be that of a dry leaf.
Think of home. Think of your roots. (A dry leave falls off the tree never to return).

305. I have sent a fish to the stream.
A messenger who may not likely return because s/he has gone to where s/he rightly belongs.

306. Do not spend you life like a snail.
Do not be slow, without property, and moving along with all that you possess.

307. The eye does not shoot a bird.
You can peep or look, but that is all there is to it. You cannot enjoy any part of it.

308. The hawk said it was necessary that old people should not all die, lest the younger generation take it for their meat (the hawk is not eaten).
This last saying is usually used in applause of what an elderly person has said. By this it is intended that wisdom resides with the old.

Select Bali Nyonga Fables

309. When a man caught a pangolin, he did not know how to kill it. He brought it home. He heard singing within the vicinity. He went there, took the rattle, tuned

a song and in the song he asked the question "what do you do when you catch a pangolin?". In the chorus somebody answered that you boil water and put the pangolin inside. The man left and did just that.

310. In a certain village, there were lots of complaints of theft. The Fon was helpless. One day he conceived a plan. He called all his subjects to the piazza. When they were assembled, the Fon got up, took his spear and with an angry expression, he told the people that the stealing had become notorious. He wanted to kill the thief. As he was thus saying he took aim inside the crowd and the thief took to his heels. By this the thief was known and caught.

311. A man with three wives wanted to find out the extent of their love for him. He took a clay pot, concocted some herbs and put inside. He placed the pot under his bed. He called his three wives and told them that his life depended on that pot and that if anybody touched the pot he the man would die. Not long he had a problem with the third wife, the first thing she did was to go and carry the pot and shatter it outside. He now knew their minds.

312. A father stole a hen and put inside his bag. Some children saw him so they were running after him shouting. Thief fowl! Thief fowl! This father was so embarrassed and ashamed. So when he met an old man he asked him to look inside the bag with an old man's eyes and see whether there is any fowl in it. The old man looked with an old man's eyes and did not see any fowl. So he scolded the children for falsely accusing their father of theft. He told them that he had looked inside the bag with an old man's eyes and did not see any fowl. True to the saying that what an old man may see sitting,

a young man cannot see even standing. Hence it is not all that the eye sees which the mouth must proclaim.

313. When hot water was thrown on the bedbug with its children, the children were wailing and writhing in pain. The bug comforted its children with these words. "Do not cry, for whatever is hot will surely get cold".

314. The hen told its chicks, "my children, you see that as I scatter the soil foraging for food, I never once look back. What is past is past. I look only ahead for better things lie ahead".

Part Two

SELECTION OF AFRICAN PROVERBS

1. Wisdom is like a baobab tree; a single person's hand cannot embrace it.
   Akan and Ewe (Ghana).
2. I pointed out to you the stars (the moon) and all you saw was the tip of my finger.
   Sukuma (Tanzania)
3. The unfortunate cow has to stay outside in the rain while the dog stays inside the house at the fireplace.
   Sukuma (Tanzania)
4. When elephants fight the grass gets hurt.
   Swahili, East Africa.
5. Better a curtain hanging motionless than a flag blowing in the wind.
   Source unknown
6. One who keeps saying "I will listen (obey)" will be cooked with the corn cob.
   Source unknown
7. No problem, the real thing will happen later. We are still young, let us enjoy life.
   Source unknown
8. Two roads overcome the hyena, and a dog can't guard two villages.
   Source unknown
9. To lose the way is to learn the way (Swahili); to give is to save (Swahili) and giving is not losing; it is keeping for tomorrow
   (Lozi, Zambia)
10. Unity is strength; division is weakness.
    Sukuma, Tanzania
11. The hen with chicks doesn't swallow the worm.
    Sukuma, Tanzania

12. What goes into the stomach is not lasting.
Sukuma, Tanzania
13. To make marks on the trees.
Source unknown
14. No matter how skinny, the son always belongs to the father.
Kenya
15. I am because we are; we are because I am.
Source unknown
16. A person is a person through other people
Source unknown
17. There is always room for the person you love even if the house is crowded.
Sukuma
18. Those who love each other don't tread on each other's toes.
Source unknown
19. It takes a whole village to raise a child.
Source unknown
20. One fingernail does not crush a louse
Ganda.
21. One finger does not kill a flea.
Maasi, Kenya/Tanzania
22. Many beads form one necklace.
Luo, Kenya
23. Many pieces of firewood keep the fire burning until the morning.
Sukuma
24. When spider webs unite, they can tie up a lion.
Amharic, Ethiopia
25. Enough spider webs wound together can stop a lion.
Source unknown
26. When they are together, strings of barks can tie up an

elephant.
Oromo, Ethiopia

27. One who encounters problems in a crowd will be helped.
Kaonde, Zambia
28. To put a roof on top of the walls of a hut needs the joining of hands.
Shona, Zimbabwe
29. A red calabash becomes more redder because of passing it from one person to another.
Kamba, Kenya
30. Neighbors share meat; they help each other like white ants.
31. To stay together is fraternity.
Tonga, Zambia.
32. Teeth without gaps chew the meat.
Ganda
33. Not to aid one in distress is to kill him or her in your heart.
34. It is a pain and curse to be alone.
Akan
35. Life is when you are with others; alone you are like an animal.
Chewa
36. Carve with your friend; alone you cut yourself.
Luvale, Zambia
37. The sterile woman has nobody to help her.
Sukuma
38. The tears of an orphan fall on his/her own knees.
Lunda, Zambia
39. Treat the earth well. It was not given to you by your parents; it was loaned to you by your children.
Source unknown

40. A house built by God does not collapse.
 Oromo
41. My heart is like a tree that only grows well where it feels at home.
42. Like ring and finger.
 Swahili.
43. Ring and finger don't separate.
 Swahili
44. The nail is never separated from the finger.
 Chewa
45. Wherever the snail goes, there goes the shell and its pouch does not separate.
 Sukuma
46. Together like basket and food.
 Ganda
47. You have been heart and soul with me as Nnalunga was with Jju
48. One stick may smoke but it will not burn.
 Oromo
49. One piece of firewood does not make the pot boil.
 Chewa
50. A good supply of wood keeps the fire burning through the night.
 Source unknown
51. You never let the home fire go out.
 Source unknown
52. As long as there is a fire burning in a village, so long as God will give us light.
 Source unknown
53. The three stones that support the cooking pot are cold.
 Source unknown
54. Where there are many people God is there.
 Source unknown

55. The hoe does not deceive.
Sukuma
56. The hoe has finished my relatives.
Sukuma
57. What goes into the stomach is not lasting. The things of this world are not lasting. Only a person who is alive eats. A dead person does not eat
Sukuma
58. When your turn has come, fold your sleeping mat
Ankole/Kiga, Uganda.
59. The corpse washer is washed in his or her turn
Swahili.
60. You can run away from the rain sickness, but you cannot run away from the dew death.
Sukuma.
61. Death's cutlass does not weed or clear only one individual.
Source unknown
62. God swallows us up and doesn't spit us out again. Death is at everyone's door.
Sukuma
63. If the Supreme Being has not killed you, even if a human being attempts to kill you, you will not die.
Akan.
64. God never dies; only people do.
Central African Republic
65. The person who was broken knows how to bind up another who is broken.
Oromo.
66. The powerful hero is a single person, but all kill the lion.
Kaoude.
67. When the elephant dies, everyone goes with their knives.

Sukuma

68. God is the real physician.
    Swahili East Africa
69. If you do not fill up a crack, you will have to build a wall.
    Source unknown
70. The one who bewitch you is a member of your family.
    Sukuma
71. He who eats with you kills you.
    Sukuma
72. People cure, God heals.
    Akan
73. It is God who drives away flies from the animal without a tail.
    Source unknown
74. It is God who pounds the "fufu" of the one armed person.
    Source unknown
75. It is God who drives away flies from the back of the tailless cow.
    Edo, Nigeria
76. God cleans the millet of the blind person.
    Source unknown
77. Reconciliation is deeper in eating together.
    A logir Ethnic group, Sudan.
78. A wise person who knows proverbs reconciles difficulties.
    Yoruba
79. Telling the story of healing and the healing power of telling the story.
    Source unknown
80. The person who has not travelled widely thinks his or her mother is the only cook (the best cook).

Ganda and Kamba.

81. One who never travels thinks it is only his or her mother who is a good cook.
Kikuyu.
82. The child who does not leave home praises his or her mother's cooking as the best.
Bemba.
83. The one who does not travel thinks his or her mother's soup is the best.
Akan and Gurune (Ghana)
84. By staying in the same place one gets lice
Source unknown
85. The person whose feet feel the morning dew is better than the person who remains at the fireplace
Source unknown
86. A crocodile's young do not grow in one pool.
Chewa
87. The salesperson does not have only one door.
Sukuma
88. Travelling is learning
Kikuyu.
89. Travelling is seeing
Kikuyu/Shona.
90. Those who travel see much
Sukuma/Swahili.
91. One who does not move about knows very little
Haya
92. A person who goes fishing never passes by a stream without trying to spear a few fish.
Sukuma
93. What causes one to give up a job is another job.
Sukuma
94. A blacksmith builds alongside the road so that he or she

may get advice.
Ganda

95. To be called is to be sent. We are not only called but also sent.
Swahili
96. The clever person is not overcome by difficulties.
Sukuma
97. People who remove honey from a beehive are always two
Source unknown
98. Two people can take a splinter out of an eye
Kimbu.
99. When spider webs unite, they catnip up a lion. The voice of many is heard by God.
Source unknown
100. Two small antelopes can beat a big one.
Source unknown
101. Relationship is in the soles of the feet
Source unknown
102. Those who discover a treasure value it more than those who are born with it.
Kuria and Ngoreme
103. The patient person eats ripe fruits
Haya.
104. The person who preserves unripe fruits eats it when it is ripe
Swahili.
105. Eyes that know how to wait put the crown on the head
Ganda.
106. Little by little the moon becomes full
Oromo.
107. One by one makes a bundle

Ganda.

108. A little rain each day will fill the river till it overflows.
Bassa/Kpelle, Liberia.

109. Slowly, slowly the rat eats the bait.
Kuria/Ngoreme/Sukuma.

110. Slowly, slowly is the way to pour porridge into the ground
Kuria/Ngoreme.

111. One who sees something good must narrate it.
Ganda

112. The one who does not risk leaving something behind will find nothing.
Kikuyu

113. A real person goes beyond himself or herself.
Sukuma

114. The ant tries to eat the rock.
Sukuma

115. A little hidden, even compatible path is the one that leads to the highway.
Kikuyu

116. It was the mad person who saw the enemy approaching.
Chewa

117. Two roads overcome the hyena.
Luyia, Lango; Uganda.

118. If we stop reaching out we die.
Source unknown

119. All that is not given is lost.
Source unknown

120. You only have what you give away.
Source unknown

121. Giving is not losing; it is keeping for tomorrow.

Source unknown

122. To give is to save. Sharing is wealth.
Source unknown

123. That which is good is never finished.
Sukuma, Tanzania.

124. When you are thirsty in the desert, follow the birds, they will lead you to water.
Namibia

125. Do not instruct someone who will not listen to you.
Ancient Egypt.

126. He that will not be counseled cannot be helped.
Uganda

127. No one person is completely wise.
Yoruba, Nigeria

128. Other people's wisdom prevents a chief from being called a fool.
Nigeria

129. When a person drinks palm wine, he does not remain quiet.
Akan, Ghana

130. A small pot boils quickly.
Swahili, Tanzania

131. Though the case may be serious, one should not strike with an axe.
Akan, Ghana

132. The teeth that laugh are also those that bite.
Hausa, Nigeria

133. The eye cannot know the soup that has salt in it.
Gonja, Ghana

134. A delicious stew will not last long in the pot.
Yoruba, Nigeria

135. The usefulness of a well is known when it dries up.
Uganda

136. An adult who decides to behave like a child should be disciplined like a child.
Ibo, Nigeria

137. A blind man knows more about his environment than a foreigner who has eyes.
Source unknown

138. When a blind man shouts "I will throw a stone at you" he has a stone under his foot.
Ewe, Ghana

139. The one-eyed man thanks God only when he sees a man who is totally blind.
Nigeria

140. The one who boasts much achieves little.
Yoruba, Nigeria

141. Why go about proclaiming the merits of a thing?
Source unknown

142. Those who observe are people who can judge.
Congo

143. What one handles gently is never destroyed; it is what one handles carelessly that causes one grief.
Yoruba, Nigeria

144. If you don't want to see smoke, don't light a fire.
Gonja, Ghana.

145. If you eat on two sides (seek double advantage), you will die a premature death.
Akan, Ghana

146. One does not play with oil that is hot.
Nkundo-mungo, Congo

147. A monkey does not leap into a trap in which its pal was taken.
Nkundo-mungo, Congo

148. Do not sow groundnuts when the monkey is watching.

Akan, Ghana

149. Never give up what you've seen for what you've heard.
Swahili, Tanzania
150. When you enjoy prosperity, take heed to the time of bad luck.
Nkundo-mungo, Congo
151. If you stretch your hand forward when walking, your head will never hit a wall.
Buila, Ghana.
152. When a crocodile smiles, be extra careful.
Swahili, Tanzania.
153. When you get a gun, don't throw your bow and arrow away.
Dagarti, Ghana
154. Never throw away the old at the sight of the new.
Shona, Zimbabwe.
155. The beast that will bite you will not show you its teeth.
Ewe Ghana.
156. Wherever a man goes to live, his character follows him
Yoruba, Nigeria
157. Every man's character is good in his own eyes.
Yoruba, Nigeria
158. One does not discover the heart of a brother if one has not begged from him in want.
Egypt
159. When rain beats on leopard it wets it, but rain does not wash out its spots.
Ashanti, Ghana
160. Without children there would soon be the end of the world.

Swahili, Tanzania

161. The way you bring up children, so they will grow.
Swahili, Tanzania

162. What a child says is what he has heard at home.
Hausa, Nigeria

163. Pull out the child out of water before you punish him.
Efik, Nigeria.

164. A child of two homes may go hungry.
Ewe, Togo

165. You are the one who eats the fruits of what your father has planted.
Kikuyu, Kenya

166. One does not instruct a child on return, one instructs him when going.
Lamba, Zimbabwe

167. A child disobedient to his father and mother eats unsalted food.
Akan, Ghana

168. A child must not be prevented from going to the farm at dusk; for when he can no longer see due to the darkness, he will return home.
Ewe, Ghana

169. For the child who dances well, it is the father's name that people ask and not the child's name.
Ewe, Ghana

170. An elderly man does not watch children's play turn into a fight.
Ewe, Togo

171. A child makes a bow from the same tree that his father uses.
Ewe, Ghana

172. He who asks questions cannot avoid answers.

Cameroon

173. One does not deride a diseased person; the fate that has befallen him today might befall you tomorrow.
Akan, Ghana.

174. If you do what you should not do, you will see what you should not see.
Source unknown

175. Whatever a person does will one day affect him.
Ibo, Nigeria

176. A person who habitually says "I do not ask others", is not wise.
Source unknown

177. If they unite, ants can kill an elephant.
Yoruba, Nigeria

178. The small ants says "nothing beats a crowd"
Liberia

179. The coward who stays at home from battle subjects himself to the ridicule and mockery of women.
Akan, Ghana.

180. If you lose your culture, you lose your sole identity.
Ewe , Togo

181. Death does not book an appointment.
Ewe , Togo

182. When the cat dies the mice celebrates.
Ewe, Ghana

183. A tsetsefly has no one to mourn him.
Akan, Ghana

184. Many are killed by folly, but none is killed by caution.
Yoruba, Nigeria

185. A parent dies in the body, but not in the minds of the children.
Ganda, Uganda

186. When death kills your contemporary, it is a warning to yourself.
Yoruba, Nigeria
187. A debtor who borrows to pay his debt is still a debtor.
Ibo, Nigeria
188. While making a loan to somebody you may be in a sitting posture; but to demand the loan back you have to get up.
Ganda, Uganda
189. A man of sound judgment cannot be deceived.
Tsonga, Zimbabwe
190. What the eyes have seen is what the eyes go after.
Ewe, Ghana
191. Whoever is destined to prosper cannot be stopped.
Source unknown
192. A person destined for glory never suffers disgrace; a powerful horse is favored among horses.
Yoruba, Nigeria
193. Nothing is more painful than disgrace.
Akan, Ghana.
194. Do not prefer death to life in misfortune out of despair.
Ancient Egypt
195. Dreaming comes prior to getting.
Mamprusi, Ghana
196. The head which has dreams is superior.
Akan, Ghana
197. For the wise child one lesson suffices.
Nkundo-Mungo, Congo
198. A man learns from what happens to him.
Ewe, Ghana
199. The best talent is a sharp ear and a good memory.

Kenya

200. Learning is like sailing the ocean; no one has ever seen it whole.
Swahili, Tanzania

201. What you have seen you know. What you have not seen, you must believe.
Namibia

202. Education has no end.
Swahili, Tanzania

203. Learning is light that leads into everything lovely.
Swahili, Tanzania

204. Wealth, if you use it, comes to an end; learning, if you use it, increases.
Swahili, Tanzania

205. When a stupid man becomes educated, a wise man finds himself in difficulties.
Swahili, Tanzania

206. Courtesy is a hallmark of education.
Swahili, Tanzania

207. Here are two ears you have, let them listen.
Lamba, Zimbabwe

208. A tree that has been crooked for thirty years cannot be straightened in one day.
Mamprusi, Ghana

209. The river grows larger because of its tributaries.
Nkundo-Mungo, Congo

210. The crooked hoe handle cannot be straightened.
Builsa, Ghana

211. Progress depends on one's effort.
Haya, Tanzania

212. If you try your best you come out victorious.
Akan, Ghana

213. If you don't try to shoot you hit nothing.

Owambo, Angola

214. A new thing does not come to him who sits, but to him who travels.
Oshona, Mozambique

215. The one who loses an enemy does not cry after him.
Wolof, Gambia

216. A miserable man has no enemies.
Akan, Ghana

217. The person who is not on good terms with you should not be sent into the bush to collect herbs for you when you are ill.
Akan, Ghana

218. A tree which is not taller than you cannot shade you.
Wolof, Gambia

219. He, who commits evil, expects evil.
Guinea

220. When you dig a pit of evil, do not make it deep.
Fulani, Nigeria

221. If you see evil and say nothing against it, it will destroy you.
Ewe, Ghana

222. Evil deeds are like perfume: difficult to hide.
Yoruba, Nigeria

223. When a man is setting out to do evil, advice is a joke to him.
Akan, Ghana

224. Not evil, but only good will last.
Kikuyu, Kenya

225. Smoke (evil) cannot be hidden.
Burundi

226. If the leader does not walk straight, those who follow him will do the same.

Tsonga, Mozambique

227. If one person eats all the honey, he is sure to get a belly-ache.
Akan, Ghana

228. The cutting grass does not attend a market of dogs.
Source unknown

229. We all start as stupid and become wise; thanks to experience.
Tanzania

230. The hand does not miss its way into the mouth in the dark.
Ewe, Ghana

231. The unprotected town has never had enemies.
Rwanda

232. Its is not the trap that counts, but the art of trapping.
Kikuyu, Kenya

233. If you don't carry me, you will not know how heavy I am.
Mamprusi, Ghana

234. A travelled child knows better than an old man who sits at home.
Ibo, Nigeria

235. If you plant corn and falsehood, falsehood comes up first.
Akan, Ghana

236. If you sow falsehood, you will harvest deceit.
Akan, Ghana

237. What is famous does not last.
Swahili, Tanzania

238. A blacksmith gains fame only when his tools and weapons prove satisfactory.
Nkundo-Mungo, Congo

239. The fence around a house conceals the secrets of the household.
Source unknown

240. One cannot hear a brother's cry and say one is busy.
Ibo, Nigeria

241. Your eyes and nose will tell you if the house is good.
Dama, Namibia

242. Dispute between brothers does not have to be settled by the chief.
Masia, Tanzania

243. Only a fool hates his family.
Hausa, Nigeria

244. God gave us the seed of every plant, but we have to sow it.
Congo

245. The farmer is one, but those who eat are many.
Swahili, Tanzania

246. If the farmer did not cultivate crops, the scholars would not be able to study.
Tanzania

247. He who will not cultivate his field will die of hunger.
Guinea

248. Nice words will not produce food.
Nigeria

249. To till the land is to love oneself.
Kikuyu, Kenya

250. The farm of the endless talker never produces much.
Akan, Ghana

251. If you are taller than your father it does not follow that he is your equal.
Akan, Ghana

252. Faults are a hill; you mount your own, and see the

other people's (faults).
Hausa, Nigeria

253. He, who does not see his own vices, should not take notice of the faults of his companions.
Swahili, Tanzania

254. When fear enters, truth escapes.
Swahili, Tanzania

255. It is the hen with chicken that fears the hawk.
Akan, Ghana

256. When a porcupine is prepared to fight, its quills will tell.
Akan, Ghana

257. The strength of a ram depends not so much on its horns as on its fighting spirit.
Akan, Ghana

258. The strength of the battle is wisdom.
Nkundo-Mungo, Congo

259. A small fire destroys a big forest.
Haya, Tanzania

260. Do not kindle a fire that you cannot put out.
Swahili, Tanzania

261. Bad water also quenches the fire.
Mamprusi, Ghana

262. The wood that was touched by fire is not difficult to ignite again.
Akan, Ghana

263. One stick cannot make a fire.
Gonja, Ghana

264. The heat of fire is better enjoyed from a considerable distance.
Akan, Ghana

265. One piece of wood does not keep the fire alive.
Kikuyu, Kenya

266. Frying, boiling and parching hear news of fire but roasting sees fire face to face.
Hausa, Nigeria

267. Never rust the people who flatter you.
Akan, Ghana

268. The leopard said: if you rest, you eat your tail (from want).
Liberia

269. Tasty food is not necessarily good food.
Zulu, South Africa

270. If you ask that cow cooked for your breakfast, than what will be used for your soup at lunch?
Akan, Ghana

271. A hen said : it is easy to find, but hard to get away to a place where you can eat it in peace.
Hausa, Nigeria

272. A child who never travelled said that only his mother knows how to cook delicious food
Ewe, Togo

273. To eat too much leaves you with swollen stomach.
Kikuyu, Kenya

274. When a fool is cursed, he thinks he is being praised.
Ethiopia

275. Only a fool drinks water from the well of envy.
Hausa, Nigeria

276. Only a fool believes everything he is told.
Kunama, Eritrea

277. A fool does not see danger even when told.
Owambo, Nigeria

278. You can beat a fool half to death, but you cannot beat his foolishness out of him.
Ewe Ghana

279. A warning to the wise is a blessing, to the fool an

insult.
Swahili, Tanzania

280. One who claps hands for a fool to dance is no better than the fool.
Yoruba, Nigeria

281. He who does not consider the outcome will end with an "if I had known"
Swahili, Tanznia

282. Prepare now for the solution of tomorrow's problems.
Swahili, Tanzania

283. Look at the other side of the log(before jumping over).
Swahili, Tanzania

284. Being prepared before-hand is better than afterthought.
Kanuri, Nigeria

285. It is because of forgetfulness that there is a reminder.
Ewe, Togo

286. Medicine for shame is forgiveness.
Bambara, Mali

287. He who does not know how to forgive, let him not expect to be forgiven.
Swahili, Tanzania

288. If you affend someone, ask for forgiveness; if offended forgive.
Ethiopia

289. He who forgives gains victory in dispute (or ends it).
Yoruba, Nigeria

290. When fortune knocks at the door, you have to open the door yourself.
Swahili, Tanzania

291. Good fortune will not happen to you: good fortune is given to him who seeks it.
Ancient Egypt

292. To be without a friend means to be poor indeed.
Somalia

293. A close friend may become your enemy.
Ethiopia

294. Misfortune will examine the sincerity of your friends and neighbours.
Akan, Ghana

295. Among friends there are some who are greater friends than others.
Akan, Ghana

296. Friendship can neither be bought nor sold.
Morocco

297. You have many friends as long as you are prosperous.
Baganda, Uganda

298. Friendship begins with meeting on a road.
Kikuyu, Kenya

299. Many friends make one's pocket empty.
Kikuyu, Kenya

300. Friendship is stronger than kinship.
Ganda, Uganda

301. You know your true friend when you are in trouble.
Akan, Ghana

302. Being uncritical does not make for good friendship.
Ghana

303. A friend is the one who praises you when you are not there.
Yoruba, Nigeria

304. Friends know you when you are prosperous and you know them when you are in adversity.

Swahili, Tanzania

305. Giving to a friend is not the same like throwing away, it is a reserve for the future.
Swahili, Tanzania

306. He who does not advice you is not your friend.
Owambo, Angola

307. It is easier to lose a friend than to find one again.
Swahili, Tanzania

308. The house-bound child will not have friends.
Uganda

309. Do not worry about tomorrow.
South Africa

310. You should see what is before you, not what is behind you.
Kanuri, Niger

311. We use foreign brains to develop our future.
Fanti, Ghana

312. He who receives a gift does not measure it.
Kenya

313. God's gifts are greater than human gifts.
Akan, Ghana

314. A man who has wealth can still receive gifts.
Ewe, Togo

315. To give is to save.
Owambo, Angola

316. Giving hands receive.
Uganda

317. What you give, you take ten times over.
Yoruba, Nigeria

318. He who gives to you, stores, he who refuses you, buries.
Uganda

319. He who trusts in God does not lack anything.

Swahili, Tanzania

320. If you have forgotten God, you have forgotten yourself.
Swahili, Tanzania

321. A mortal owns the saying and God owns the fulfillment.
Swahili, Tanzania

322. God loves him who cares for the poor more than him who respects the wealthy.
Ancient Egypt

323. If you want to tell anything to the Supreme Being, tell it to the wind.
Akan, Ghana

324. What God gives one does not refuse. One receives it gladly.
Lamba, Zimbabwe

325. Allah is the cure for all (ills).
Hausa, Nigeria

326. The truly contented man becomes from Allah.
Hausa, Nigeria

327. When a man recovers from sickness, he forgets God.
Ethiopia

328. Good luck means to follow God's will.
Egypt

329. When a man is in difficulty then he remembers God.
Nigeria

330. God gives many things, but only ones.
Burundi

331. God is the source of all life.
Akan, Ghana

332. One does not trade in partnership with God and

incur a loss.
Yoruba, Nigria

333. A habitual errand refuse cannot refuse God's errand.
Yoruba, Nigeria

334. When a fowl drinks water, it shows it to God.
Akan, Ghana

335. Goodness is better than gold.
Akan, Ghana

336. Nobody runs away from goodness.
Akan, Ghana

337. Every good you do has its benefit.
Akan, Ghana

338. Your goodness is not for yourself but for others.
Akan, Ghana

339. A good thing sells itself.
Akan, Ghana

340. It is tiredness that makes resting enjoyable.
Yoruba, Nigeria.

341. One does a kind deed to store it and not as a gift.
Akan, Ghana

342. When one gets a boil on ones' forehead; one cannot hide it from the public.
Ewe, Togo

343. Nobody can see his own goodness; it can be seen only by others.
Kikuyu, Kenya

344. An elder pays no attention to rumors.
Akan, Ghana

345. A bad temper kills its owner.
Akan, Ghana

346. Gossip is trouble's predecessor.
Akan, Ghana

347. Gossiping and lying are siblings.

Kenya

348. Gossip, even if it is true, creates disharmony.
Akan, Ghana

349. We are grateful for the blossoms when we eat the fruits.
Shona, Zimbabwe

350. The ass's gratitude is farting.
Swahili, Tanzania

351. How many cured patients remember their doctor?
Egypt

352. If one who receives help is ungrateful, he gets no help again.
Ibo, Nigeria

353. You have cured his testicles and he has used them on your wife.
Uganda

354. Do not despise a bridge you have crossed.
Swahili, Tanzania

355. Ingratitude is the world's reward.
South Africa

356. Ingratitude is the worst sin.
North Africa

357. Ingratitude shown to helper deserves a punishment.
Akan, Ghana

358. He whom you teach to cultivate does not give you anything of what he grows in abundance.
Ganda, Uganda

359. Greatness is achieved by effort.
Hausa, Nigeria

360. You only realize the full length of a frog when it is dead.
Ewe, Ghana

361. If we stand tall it is because we stand on the backs

of those who come
Ewe, Ghana

362. You do not become a chief by sitting on a big stool.
Ewe, Ghana

363. Greed for the things of this world will keep the soul out of paradise.
Sudan

364. Do not take another mouthful before you have swallowed what is in your mouth.
Madagascar

365. If one person eats all the honey, it purges his stomach.
Akan, Ghana

366. One who sets too many traps will find some animals decaying.
Nkundo-Mungo, Congo

367. The monkey ate with two hands and fell from the tree.
Liberia

368. Returning a second time led to a thief's capture.
Swahili, Tanzania

369. A guest is like a fish: after three days he is no longer fresh.
South Africa

370. A guest is a guest today. Tomorrow give him a hoe.
Swahili, Tanzania

371. A guest is like a river: he should not be stagnant.
Kikuyu, Kenya

372. If you hear "welcome", you will also hear "may you reach your home safely".
Akan, Ghana

373. A happy heart is more than anything else.
Akan, Ghana

374. Happiness is to follow the will of God.
Egypt

375. If you don't find happiness at home, you will not find it beyond the borders.
Swahili, Tanzania

376. To live a happy life, you must be modest in life.
Fon, Benin

377. Happiness requires something to do, something to love and something to hope for.
Swahili, Tanzania

378. To feel hatred in one's heart is worse than to suffer poverty.
Guinea

379. The path to God is the path to health.
Swahili, Tanzania

380. A healthy person does not seek a doctor.
Nkundo-Mungo, Congo

381. Health has no price.
Mamprusi, Ghana

382. The doctor cannot drink the medicine for the patient.
Akan, Ghana

383. There is no medicine as active as good food.
Ibo, Nigeria

384. Do no scorn the remedy that you can use.
Ancient Egypt

385. It is the heart that carries one to hell or to heaven.
Kanuri, Nigeria

386. Follow your heart and you perish.
Akan, Ghana

387. A man's face shows what is in his heart.
Hausa, Nigeria

388. If you want to hear the news of the heart ask the

face.
Fulani, Nigeria

389. What the heart desires is like medicine to it.
Swahili, Tanzania

390. What is stored in the heart does not rot.
Uganda

391. The help you give to others will soon be your own help.
Kikuyu, Kenya

392. The decline and fall of a state begins in the homes of its people.
Akan, Ghana

393. Home affairs must not go into the open.
Kikuyu, Kenya

394. The house is for sleeping by night, not for staying in by day.
Kikuyu, Kenya

395. A slanderer has no peaceful home.
Kikuyu, Kenya

396. Among many sympathizers only a few are sincere.
Akan, Ghana

397. Slowness is sometimes more advantageous than speed.
Akan, Ghana

398. One tree does not bear the fruits of another tree.
Ewe, Togo

399. He who sleeps in a room knows where it leaks.
Gonja, Ghana.

400. A noisy man is harmless.
Swahili, Tanzania.

401. We have no idea how heavy is a load which we are not lifting
Source unknown

402. A dog who has honey, people call "Mr dog".
Source unknown
403. Never look into the eyes of a crying man.
Source unknown
404. A tree without leaves becomes firewood
Ghana.
405. Even the land can become infertile
Yoruba, Nigeria.
406. A guest does not eat as much as he wants
Kikuyu, Kenya.
407. Each time an old man dies, it is as if a library got burnt.
Senegal
408. What makes the drum pleasing is the song.
Lamba, Zimbabwe.
409. The most important things are left in the locker.
Kikuyu, Kenya
410. If someone promises you a pair of trousers, you should check if he has a pair of shorts.
Dangame, Ghana
411. One who cooks his own food does not beg.
Kikuyu, Kenya.
412. The one who gives you a fish at high water season is a true friend.
Nkundo-Mungo, Congo.
413. A snake does not bite a child in front of his mother.
Ewe, Togo
414. A good chief is like a food basket. He keeps the people together.
Dama
415. What a cat saw and closed its eyes, a dog did not see it before barking.
Ewe, Togo

416. Whoever catches a hare has to run for it.
Hausa, Nigeria

417. If an opportunity is not taken, it passes away.
Akan, Ghana

418. When you know who his friend is, you know who he is.
Senegal

419. A stray pet is easily stolen
Akan, Ghana

420. Disreputable traders deserve disreputable customers
Akan, Ghana

421. No one chases two birds at once.
Ewe, Ghana.

422. The Sheppard's staff does not kill the sheep
Ewe, Ghana

423. It is easy to become a monk in one's old age
Ethiopia.

424. A busy road has no weeds.
Akan, Ghana.

425. The law of fishes: the big ones eat the small ones.
Swahili, Tanzania.

426. I f you are honored, do not dishonor yourself
Akan, Ghana.

427. Everybody must take the consequences of his action.
Hausa, Nigeria

428. All the fingers are not equal.
Ga, Ghana.

429. What lowers itself is ready to fall
Wolof, Gambia.

430. You most look left and right before you whisper.
Fon, Benin

431. People do not value that which costs them nothing.
Kikuyu, Kenya

432. The rainy season which is going to be a good one is known when the first rain falls.
Hausa, Nigeria

433. Arguments are the source of strife.
Kikuyu, Kenya.

434. Similar characters make a friendship
Yoruba, Nigeria.

435. Hardship reveals personality.
Swahili, Tanzania.

436. If your yard is nice it is due to your own effort.
Ghana

437. If two people carry a log, it does not press hard on their heads.
Akan, Ghana

438. If you are cruel, no one wants to settle with you.
Kikuyu, Kenya.

439. If you want to keep your workmen, keep your temper.
South Africa

440. When you have, give.
Owambo, Namibia

441. Take care that you don't make the wolf your shepherd.
South Africa

442. A tall tree catches all the wind.
Source unknown

443. Other people's misfortune is easy to bear
Malawi.

444. Nobody should ask a fish what is happening on the land. And nobody should ask a rat what is happening in water
Yoruba, Nigeria

445. If two people set a trap together, they go to check it

together.
Ewe, Togo

446. For a king to be a king, he must be supported
Fon, Benin.

447. If there is no elephant, the buffalo would be considered the biggest animal.
Akan, Togo

448. The hen knows it is dawn, but it leaves the announcement to the cockerel.
Akan, Ghana

449. Do not force a big thread into a bead with a small hole.
Kikuyu, Kenya

450. To stay together is to know each other.
Kikuyu, Kenya

451. Man counts what he is refused, not what he is given.
Kikuyu, Kenya

452. If you want to insult somebody, remember that you may need salt one day.
Benin

453. If you eat from the same plate with bad eaters, you will have your hands dirtied by soup.
Fon, Benin

454. He who has no teeth should not hate the one who is chewing meat.
Fon, Benin

455. The redeemer of people is a walker with people.
Lambo, Zimbabwe

456. If you are ushered in to a sitting room, you should not enter a bedroom.
Fon, Benin

457. Because friendship is pleasant, we partake of our friend's entertainment, not because we have not enough

food to eat in our house.
Yoruba, Nigeria

458. We cannot dwell in a house together without speaking to one another.
Yoruba, Nigeria

459. If somebody provides you with the ear, you provide him with the eye.
Ewe, Togo

460. When you go to the country of snails, you do not ask them for a bedroom.
Ewe, Togo

461. A needle does not look for a thread; it is the thread that looks for the needle.
Ewe, Togo

462. To be dead is better than to alive and not be respected.
Ewe, Ghana

463. The way to welcome cold is to warm each other.
Tonga, South Africa

464. One only seeks a guide when one has lost the road.
Hausa, Nigeria

465. Relations are like a part of your body, if anything touches it, however small you feel it.
Hausa, Nigeria.

466. A man's relations are the most pleasant things on earth.
Hausa, Nigeria

467. I refuse to chew it for you; do you think I swallow it?
Hausa, Nigeria

468. If you are too playful with your dog it licks your mouth.
Akan, Ghana

469. It is the broken calabash that is mended.
Ga, Ghana.

470. Even though your eye brow is smaller, it is older than the beard.
Ewe, Togo

471. If you see your neighbor's beard in flames, you must get water beside you.
Ewe, Togo

472. He who is satisfied does not cook for the hungry.
Ewe, Togo

473. He who is yet to cross the river does not insult a crocodile.
Ewe, Togo

474. You can live as a stranger among the indigenous people, but you can never become one of them.
Ga, Ghana.

475. The ram that defecates thinks it is spoiling the path for the people, but it is spoiling its own legs.
Ewe, Togo.

476. The cook says "we are fighting but we are watching our eyes".
Ewe, Togo

477. If your sister is among the group of praise singing girls, your name is never forgotten.
Akan, Ghana.

478. If you trample upon what belongs to someone in hope of finding what belongs to you, you will never find it.
Akan, Ghana.

479. One does not strive to save other people's head and leave one's head for the kite to snatch.
Yoruba, Nigeria.

480. He who enters into friendship with a leopard will

eventually find a claw in his neck.
Nkundo-Mungo, Congo.

481. He, who lives with an ass, makes noise like an ass.
Source unknown

482. Absence makes the heart forget
Kenya.

483. Good fellowship is sharing good things with your friend.
Akan, Ghana

484. What you do secretly, others see secretly.
Akan, Ghana.

485. If you want to stay in a place, watch your conduct.
Akan, Ghana

486. If someone claims that he excels you, let him do so, for there is someone else who also excels him.
Akan, Ghana.

487. Hearing and asking promotes good relationship.
Akan, Ghana

488. One does not carry a person who keeps biting him.
Nkundo-Mungo, Congo

489. To the person who does a favour to you, show some favour in return.
Nkundo –Mungo, Congo

490. We leave bent twigs as way marks.
Nkundo –Mungo, Congo.

491. If you say that something bad should happen. to your friend, that same evil will happen to you.
Builsa, Ghana

492. It is better for you to say" I will not wrestle" than to say "let me get up".
Ewe, Ghana

493. You don't beg from the broken pot.
Builsa, Ghana

494. He who is despised will one day be admired.
Kenya.

495. Benevolence should be extended to a victim who greatly needs it.
Akan, Ghana

496. If you love your neighbour more than yourself, he mistakes you to be his servant
Akan, Ghana.

497. It better to travel alone than with a bad companion.
Senegal

498. Do not tell the man who is carrying you that he stinks.
Sierra Leone

499. Confiding a secret to an unworthy person is like carrying grain in a bag with a hole.
Ethiopia.

500. If your servants are afraid of you, they will not win victory for you.
Akan, Ghana

501. The person who does not wish his neighbour well does not prosper.
Akan, Ghana

502. The prosperity of man depends upon his fellow men.
Akan, Ghana

503. Nobody will bring a pig to a hyena for safekeeping.
Ewe, Ghana

504. Don't pride yourself with what others have accomplished.
Source unknown

505. Pride yourself with your own success.
Ewe, Ghana

506. If you want to attract someone, you should like him.

Ewe, Ghana

507. If you allow them to tie you up, you should also consent that they should pull you.
Akan, Ghana.

508. Overabundance for some means suffering for others.
Akan, Ghana

509. A leopard ate the person who was feeding him.
Zulu

510. Two birds were quarrelling over one grain of maize when the third one came and stole it from them.
Congo.

511. If you keep company with thieves, you will become a thief.
Congo

512. A man should have as a companion somebody who is older than he is.
Wolof, Gambia

513. No one can boast of what belongs to another.
Akan, Ghana

514. There is always some trouble after the stranger departs.
Akan, Ghana

515. Trampling on another's right to seek your own ends in disappointment.
Akan, Ghana

516. Do good, and it leaves in your descendants; do evil, and it lives in them likewise.
Akan, Ghana.

517. Before healing others, heal yourself.
Wolof, Gambia.

518. He who bumps into another person teaches him to be stronger.
Yoruba, Nigeria

519. If each brick says to one another" I don't want you to be put on top of me", a house would never be built.
Yoruba, Nigeria.

520. A blind man does not show the way to a blind man.
Ewe, Ghana

521. The one who deceives another is not worthy to be trusted.
Yoruba, Nigeria

522. If you associate yourself with a great man, you will advance.
Calabar, Nigeria

523. If you don't step on the tail of a dog, it will not bite you.
Cameroon

524. Cross a river with a big crowd of people and a crocodile will not eat you.
Madagascar

525. Don't try to convince somebody to dislike the person he loves, because he will continue loving that person and start hating you.
Senegal

526. Do not mend your neighbor's fence before looking to your own.
Tanzania.

527. To control oneself is better than to be controlled.
Ewe, Ghana

528. It is only when a person cannot control himself that someone else controls him.
Ewe, Ghana.

529. One cannot boast while depending on others
Ewe, Ghana.

530. If a nude person says he can dress you, don't believe him.

Akan, Ghana

531. He who deserves wine should not be given water.
Akan, Ghana

532. If you are not rich people don't value what you say.
Akan, Ghana

533. It is only when you live in abundance that people will pay you frequent visits
Fon, Benin.

534. Search people's heart before revealing your secret to them.
Fon, Benin

535. A person who is not in good health cannot cure others.
Uganda

536. A matter that concerns other people should not be kept to oneself.
Yoruba, Nigeria

537. What you don't like, don't do it to your neighbour.
Akan, Ghana

538. If you follow an elephant, you never get entangled in the forest.
Ashanti, Ghana

539. Supporting someone does not mean neglecting oneself.
Mamprusi, Ghana

540. Nobody should suffer for the delight of others.
Ewe, Ghana

541. If you are kind to others, others would be kind to you.
Ewe, Ghana

542. You should never misuse a man who did something good to you.
Source unknown

543. As a tree leans, so it falls.
Rwanda.

544. Man is like palm wine: when young, it is sweet but without strength, in the old age, it gets strong but harsh.
Congo

545. The old tree remains standing the young one.
Nkundo –Mungo, Congo

546. It is a duty of children to wait on the elders, and not the elders on children.
Kenya

547. The one who wants to rise lives near a wise man.
Zulu, South Africa

548. Old people can tell the best tales.
Swahili, Tanzania

549. A child that wears an adult's hat will have his head disappearing into it.
Ewe, Togo

550. You mock the old; soon you will be among them.
Yoruba, Nigeria

551. The old elephant knows where to find water.
South Africa

552. When the adult knows how to walk with children, the children gladly carry his travelling bag for him.
Akan, Ghana.

553. Young people cannot teach the old about traditions.
Yoruba, Nigeria

554. The youth most respect the aged, and the aged must understand the youth.
Akan, Ghana.

555. A child may dine with the elders if his hands are clean.
Akan, Ghana

556. A beard does not tell the story of the eye brow, for

the eye brow is older than the beard.
Ewe, Togo.

557. Children are not to talk on family matters
Krobo, Ghana.

558. There had been people of old before the old people were old.
Krobo, Ghana

559. You do not show the path of the forest to an old gorilla.
Akan, Ghana

Cited Works

Dzobo, N.K. 1997, *African Proverbs: The Moral Value of Ewe Proverbs,* Accra: Bureau of Ghana languages.
Healey , Joseph & Donald Sybertz', Towards an African Narrative Theology, Maryknoll, New York: Orbis Books
Ghiantar, Ngala, 1997, African Proverbs 7 Interpretations (A collection from Wimbum), Jos: Star-Link communications.
Mbiti, John S., 1969, *African Religions and Philosophy*, London: Heinemann Educational Books Ltd.
Stöckle, Johannes, 1994, *Traditions, Tales and Proverbs of Bali Nyonga,* Köln: Rüddiger Köppe Verlag,.
Tischhauser, Georg, 1994, *Mungaka Bali Dictionary*, Trans. By Johannes Stöckle, Köln: Rüddiger Köppe Verlag.

ABOUT THE AUTHOR

Babila Fochang was born in Bali, Cameroon. He has served the Presbyterian Church as pastor in various capacities and currently serves as Synod Clerk since January 2015. He holds a Master of Theology in African Christianity from the University of Kwazulu Natal (UKZN) and currently completing his doctoral dissertation at the same institution. Fochang has published extensively on Christian and moral issues from an African perspective.

Index

T

W

Y

Printed in the United States
By Bookmasters